THE ENCYCLOPI

LANDSCAPING
AND PATIO DESIGN

Over 325 ideas for LANDSCAPING AND PATIO DESIGN

RANDALL W. COLE

A visual guide to landscaping projects

ILLUSTRATIONS:
Jerry Bates
COVER:
Art Rojas

SPECIAL THANKS TO:
Dale, Doris, Amber &
Brandi Cole
Linda & Pete

Published by

Publishing

RC Publishing
1711 Newport Circle
Santa Ana, CA 92705

(714) 436-1508
Phone (800) 605-7746

The Publisher has made every effort to ensure that all illustrations given in this book are accurate and safe but cannot except liability for any resulting injury, damage or loss to either person or property whether direct or consequential and howsoever arising. The Publisher will be grateful for any information which will assist us in keeping future editions up to date.

ISBN 0-9653287-0-8

Printed in the United States of America.

Contents

Introduction

Welcome to the beautiful world of landscaping. Finally, the most comprehensive book of landscaping ideas ever published is here! This book is designed to help you create the perfect look for your home.

Like most of us, the purchase of a house is probably one of the single biggest investments you will make in your lifetime. So you strive for the best. After the purchase of your house you want to make it that special place you can call home, and landscaping is a big part of creating a comfortable and enjoyable environment for your family. So you drive around the neighborhood to get ideas of styles that will look good for your home. The only problem is that by the time you get home you can not remember exactly which ideas you liked best. Next you decide to purchase some books on landscaping which could be a very expensive proposition by the time you get everything to cover your landscaping needs.

Thank goodness for <u>The Encyclopedia of Landscaping</u>! One book giving you hundreds of ideas for all aspects of your landscaping needs. Ideas that can help you personalize your home exactly the way you visualized it. <u>The Encyclopedia of Landscaping</u> covers just about everything you could imagine from a simple mailbox or a beautiful waterfall spa to an elegant walkway or even a romantic gazebo. The ideas are endless, you can mix and match ideas and let your imagination create that perfect dream home.

Professional Landscapers are praising <u>The Encyclopedia of Landscaping</u> for its colorful and modern ideas. The feedback that we have received has been tremendous. We feel that with <u>The Encyclopedia of Landscaping</u> and your own imagination you will be able to create that perfect masterpiece for you and your family to enjoy for many years to come.

Randy Cole

Publisher and Author

LAMPPOSTS AND MAILBOXES

SQUARE DESIGNED NATURAL RIVER ROCK
Illus. 100

SQUARE CUT FLAGSTONE
Illus. 101

NATURAL FLAGSTONE
Illus. 102

**NATURAL RIVER ROCK CAPPED
WITH CONCRETE DESIGNER TOP**
Illus. 103

**RED BRICK INDENTED VERTICAL
BRICK CAPPED IN BULLNOSE**
Illus. 104

**CHARCOAL COLORED COLUMN
CAPPED IN BULLNOSE**
Illus. 105

RECTANGULAR DESIGN NATURAL RIVER ROCK
Illus. 106

STUCCO COLUMN INLAID WITH RED TILE
Illus. 107

NATURAL STACKED FLAGSTONE
Illus. 108

L-SHAPE DESIGN WITH NATURAL RIVER ROCK
Illus. 109

LOW PROFILE NATURAL FLAGSTONE
Illus. 110

**NATURAL FLAGSTONE TRIMMED WITH
BRICK AND CAPPED WITH BULLNOSE**
Illus. 111

ROUND COLUMN CAPPED IN BULLNOSE
Illus. 112

**CHARCOAL BRICK WITH STAGGERED
SQUARE CAP INLAID WITH ROCK**
Illus. 113

BROWN BRICK WITH STAGGERED CAP
Illus. 114

USED BRICK WITH STAGGERED CAP
Illus. 115

**RED BRICK WITH INDENTED VERTICAL
BRICK CAPPED IN BULLNOSE**
Illus. 116

**RED BRICK WITH VERTICAL BRICK
DESIGN CAPPED IN BULLNOSE**
Illus. 117

**RED BRICK DESIGN WITH
HERRINGBONE DESIGN CENTER**
Illus. 118

**HERRINGBONE BRICK COLUMN
CAPPED IN BULLNOSE**
Illus. 119

L-SHAPED STUCCO CAPPED IN TWO TIERED BULLNOSE
Illus. 120

CORNER STUCCO COLUMN CAPPED IN RED BRICK
Illus. 121

**STUCCO COLUMN INSET WITH BULLNOSE
CAPPED WITH DESIGNER CONCRETE**
Illus. 122

STUCCO COLUMN INSET WITH VERTICAL RED BRICK
Illus. 123

CONCRETE BLOCK WITH
BROWN BRICK INSETS
CAPPED IN BULLNOSE
Illus. 124

GEOMETRIC SHAPED CONCRETE
& STUCCO COLUMNS
Illus. 125

U-SHAPED CONCRETE CAPPED STUCCO COLUMNS
Illus. 126

11

SQUARE COLUMN INLAID WITH COLORED STUCCO
Illus. 127

STUCCO COLUMN INSIDE STUCCO PLANTER
Illus. 128

ROUND VERTICAL BRICK INLAID WITH STUCCO
Illus. 129

STACKED FLAGSTONE CAPPED IN DESIGNER CONCRETE
Illus. 130

GEOMETRIC STUCCO PORTHOLE DESIGN COLUMN
Illus. 131

GEOMETRIC STUCCO SQUARE HOLE DESIGN COLUMN
Illus. 132

STUCCO COLUMN CAPPED
IN DOUBLE CHARCOAL BULLNOSE
Illus. 133

CYLINDER STUCCO COLUMN
Illus. 134

CONCRETE & STUCCO DESIGNER COLUMN
Illus. 135

14

STRAIGHT LINE RED BRICK COLUMN CAPPED WITH DESIGNER CONCRETE
Illus. 136

STUCCO TWO TONE DESIGNER COLUMN
Illus. 137

STUCCO DESIGNER COLUMN INLAID WITH BLUE TILE
Illus. 138

DESIGNER CONCRETE & STUCCO COLUMN
Illus. 139

STUCCO COLUMN WITH THREE TIERED BRICK CAP
Illus. 140

STUCCO COLUMN CAPPED WITH DESIGNER CONCRETE
Illus. 141

WOOD SHINGLED COLUMN
Illus. 142

CONCRETE & STUCCO COLUMN INLAID WITH RED TILE
Illus. 143

WALKWAYS & PORCHES

RED BRICK TWO TIERED CURVED ENTRANCE WITH CENTER PLANTER
Illus. 144

RED BRICK HERRINGBONE PATTERN CURVED THREE TIERED ENTRANCE
Illus. 145

S-SHAPED FOUR TIERED USED BRICK WALKWAY
Illus. 146

DOUBLE LEVEL USED BRICK WALKWAY BORDERED WITH PLANTERS
Illus. 147

FLAGSTONE EDGED WITH BRICK
Illus. 148

FUNNEL STYLE ENTRANCE
Illus. 149

THREE TEIRED FLAGSTONE AND CONCRETE
Illus. 150

USED BRICK FUNNEL STYLE WALKWAY
Illus. 151

STAMPED CONCRETE TO HALF-MOON ENTRANCE
Illus. 152

FLAGSTONE STEPS ACCENTED WITH RIVER ROCK
Illus. 153

FLAGSTONE ACCENTED WITH BRICK
Illus. 154

FUNNEL STYLE ENTRANCE WITH BRICK COLUMNS
Illus. 155

QUARRY ROCK HANDRAILS WITH FLAGSTONE STEPS
Illus. 156

HALF-MOON ENTRANCE USING FLAGSTONE WALLS CAPPED IN WHITE BRICK
Illus. 157

RIGHT ANGLE USED BRICK ENTRANCE WITH CYLINDER LAMPPOSTS
Illus. 158

CHARCOAL BRICK COLUMNS INLAID WITH FLAGSTONE HANDRAILS
Illus. 159

SEMI-OPEN ENTRANCE WITH THREE LAMPPOSTS
Illus. 160

FLAGSTONE WALKWAY EDGED IN BRICK
Illus. 161

S-SHAPED HERRINGBONE PATTERN CHANGING TO SMOOTH CONCRETE EDGED IN BRICK
Illus. 162

SIMPLE RED BRICK AND CONCRETE WALKWAY
Illus. 164

HALF-MOON MULTILEVEL CONCRETE ENTRANCE
Illus. 163

STRAIGHT LINE VERTICAL CONCRETE PATTERN
Illus. 165

STAGGERED STAIRS & WALKWAY
Illus. 166

NATURAL FLAGSTONE ENTRANCE
Illus. 167

QUARRY TILE ENTRANCE WITH BUILT IN BENCH
Illus. 168

STRAIGHT RED BRICK PATTERN WITH STEPS IN BULLNOSE
Illus. 169

STRAIGHT PATTERN TILE ENTRANCE
Illus. 170

Z-SHAPED RED BRICK STEPS WITH CONCRETE WALKWAY & PORCH
Illus. 171

BASIC COLORED CONCRETE WITH BRICK EDGING
Illus. 172

S-SHAPED NATURAL FLAGSTONE WALKWAY
Illus. 173

SEMI-CIRCULAR MULTILEVEL FLAGSTONE STEPS WITH CONCRETE WALKWAY
Illus. 174

SEMI-CIRCULAR MULTILEVEL FLAGSTONE
Illus. 175

WOOD PLATFORMS SURROUNDED BY GREY ROCK ACCENTED WITH PIER PILINGS
Illus. 176

STAMPED CONCRETE WALKWAY WITH SMOOTH CONCRETE EDGING
Illus. 177

STAGGERED MULTILEVEL CONCRETE STEPS
Illus. 178

FUNNEL SHAPED WALKWAY WITH DESIGNER CONCRETE HANDRAILS
Illus. 179

SLOPING STONE HANDRAILS & LAMPPOSTS WITH THREE STEP ENTRANCE
Illus. 180

NATURAL FLAGSTONE WALKWAY & DRIVEWAY
Illus. 181

STAMPED AND SMOOTH CONCRETE
WALKWAY & ENTRANCE
Illus. 182

NATURAL FLAGSTONE WALKWAY, LAMPPOSTS
AND HANDRAILS
Illus. 183

CONCRETE WALKWAY EDGED IN BRICK
Illus. 184

**NATURAL FLAGSTONE WALKWAY WITH
SMOOTH CONCRETE CENTERS**
Illus. 185

**S-SHAPED COLORED CONCRETE EDGED
WITH CHARCOAL BRICK**
Illus. 186

S-SHAPED ENTRANCE EDGED IN BRICK
Illus. 187

S-SHAPED ENTRANCE WITH FLAGSTONE EDGED IN CONCRETE
Illus. 188

NATURAL FLAGSTONE WALKWAY
Illus. 189

HALF-MOON CHARCOAL BRICK ENTRANCE
Illus. 190

CONCRETE WALKWAY EDGED IN BRICK
Illus. 191

40

QUARRY TILE WITH CONCRETE CENTER
Illus. 192

NATURAL FLAGSTONE S-SHAPED WALKWAY WITH STACKED FLAGSTONE LAMPPOSTS
Illus. 193

COLORED CONCRETE WALKWAY EDGED IN BRICK
Illus. 194

COLORED CONCRETE WALKWAY WITH BUILT IN BRICK BENCH
Illus. 195

CONCRETE WALKWAY WITH QUARRY TILE CENTER
Illus. 196

**CURVED FLAGSTONE WALKWAY
EDGED IN BRICK**
Illus. 197

WOOD WALKWAY AND PORCH
Illus. 198

BRICK EDGED WALKWAY WITH GRAVEL CENTERS
Illus. 199

BASKET WEAVE STEPPING STONES
Illus. 200

CONCRETE STEPS SURROUNDED BY SMOOTH ROCK
Illus. 201

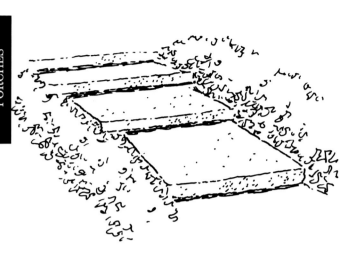

STAGGERED STEPPING STONES
Illus. 202

STAGGERED STEPS
Illus. 203

FAN FOLD STEP PATTERN
Illus. 204

DOUBLE PARALLEL STEP PATTERN
Illus. 205

PLANTERS & LAWN EDGES

V-SHAPED BRICK PLANTER
Illus. 206

GRADUATED SLOPING BRICK PATTERN
Illus. 207

SEMI-HEXAGON BRICK PATTERN
Illus. 208

ROUNDED BRICK PLANTER CAPPED WITH BULLNOSE
Illus. 209

BRICK PLANTER WITH WATERFALL AND ATTACHED LAMPPOST
Illus. 210-A

STAGGERED MULTI-STAGE BRICK PLANTER
Illus. 210-B

HILLSIDE STAGGERED BRICK PLANTER
Illus. 211

LOW PROFILE STAGGERED BRICK PLANTER
Illus. 212

SEMICIRCULAR LOW PROFILE PLANTER CAPPED WITH BULLNOSE
Illus. 213

RED BRICK PLANTER CAPPED WITH BI-LEVEL WOOD
Illus. 214

S-SHAPED STUCCO PLANTER CAPPED WITH BRICK BULLNOSE
Illus. 215

S-SHAPED STUCCO PLANTER CAPPED IN TWO TIER CONCRETE CAPS
Illus. 216

S-SHAPED STUCCO PLANTER CAPPED WITH SQUARE EDGE RED BRICK
Illus. 217

NATURAL FLAGSTONE SEMICIRCULAR PLANTER
Illus. 218

TWO TIER STUCCO PLANTER WITH LAMPPOST COLUMNS
Illus. 219

GEOMETRIC LOW PROFILE STUCCO PLANTER IN RED BRICK INCORPORATING TWO LAMPPOSTS
Illus. 220

CORNER RETAINING STUCCO PLANTER WITH SINGLE LAMPPOST
Illus. 221

TWO TIERED CORNER RETAINING PLANTER WITH SINGLE LAMPPOST
Illus. 222

L-SHAPED STACKED NATURAL FLAGSTONE PLANTER WITH ATTACHED LAMPPOST
Illus. 223

CIRCULAR SHAPED STACKED NATURAL FLAGSTONE PLANTER
Illus. 224

**SEMICIRCULAR RIVER ROCK PLANTER CAPPED WITH
CONCRETE CAPS INCORPORATING A SINGLE LAMPPOST**
Illus. 225

CORNER RIVER ROCK PLANTER WITH CONCRETE CAPS
Illus. 226

L-SHAPED NATURAL FLAGSTONE PLANTER
Illus. 227

MULTILEVEL STACKED NATURAL FLAGSTONE
Illus. 228

GEOMETRIC SHAPED NATURAL FLAGSTONE PLANTER
Illus. 229

SEMICIRCULAR NATURAL FLAGSTONE PLANTER WITH SINGLE LAMPPOST
Illus. 230

SEMICIRCULAR HIGH PROFILE NATURAL FLAGSTONE PLANTER
Illus. 231

L-SHAPED NATURAL FLAGSTONE PLANTER CAPPED IN RED BRICK
Illus. 232

STUCCO RETAINING PLANTER CAPPED IN BRICK
Illus. 233

L-SHAPED NATURAL FLAGSTONE PLANTER WITH MAILBOX POST
Illus. 234

SEMICIRCULAR STUCCO PLANTER INLAID WITH AQUA TILE
Illus. 235

GEOMETRIC MULTILEVEL STUCCO PLANTER ACCENTED WITH WOOD BEAMS
Illus. 236

NATURAL Z-SHAPED FLAGSTONE PLANTER
Illus. 237

GEOMETRIC LOW PROFILE CONCRETE STUCCO PLANTER
Illus. 238

STUCCO RETAINING PLANTER CAPPED IN RED BRICK
Illus. 239

MULTILEVEL STUCCO RETAINING WALL PLANTER CAPPED WITH BULLNOSE BRICK
Illus. 240

WALLS & FENCES

CURVED WOOD FENCE WITH RED BRICK COLUMNS CAPPED WITH DESIGNER CONCRETE
Illus. 241

ADOBE BLOCK WALL
Illus. 242

NATURAL RIVER ROCK WALL
Illus. 243

CONCRETE & STUCCO WALL WITH CONCRETE CAPS
Illus. 244

TWO COLOR DESIGNER ADOBE WALL
Illus. 245

CONCRETE & STUCCO WALL WITH DESIGNER CONCRETE CAPS
Illus. 246

MULTILEVEL STUCCO WALL CAPPED WITH COLORED BRICK
Illus. 247

WOOD LOG FENCE
Illus. 248

ADOBE BLOCK WALL WITH WROUGHT IRON INSERTS
Illus. 249

STUCCO COLUMN FENCE CAPPED WITH BRICK INCORPORATING WROUGHT IRON CENTERS
Illus. 250

STAGGERED Z-SHAPED RETAINING WALL CAPPED IN RED BRICK
Illus. 251

WOOD PIER PILINGS WALL & EDGING
Illus. 252

TWO TONE WOOD INLAID FENCE
Illus. 253

STUCCO AND DECORATOR WOOD ACCENTED WALL
Illus. 254

SPLIT STAGGERED WOOD FENCE
Illus. 255

BASKET WEAVE RED BRICK DESIGN WALL WITH LOG WOOD RETAINING PLANTER
Illus. 256

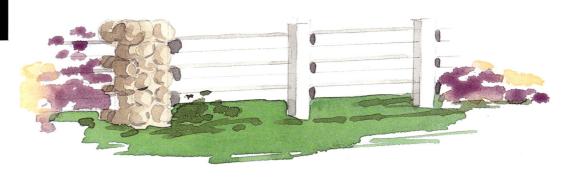

WOOD LOG FENCE WITH RIVER ROCK COLUMNS
Illus. 257

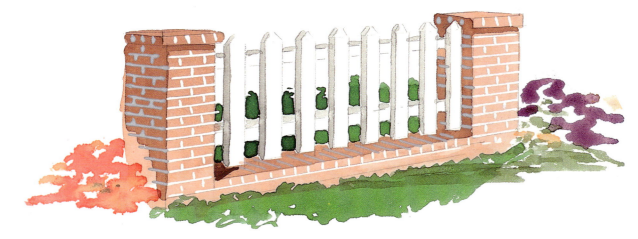

RED BRICK COLUMNS CAPPED IN BULLNOSE BRICK WITH WHITE WOOD PICKET CENTERS
Illus. 258

DESIGNER BRICK COLUMNS WITH WOOD SLATE WOOD CENTERS
Illus. 259

WOOD SHINGLE STYLE WALL
Illus. 260

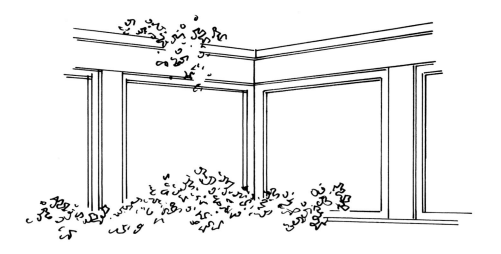

WOOD FENCE WITH DESIGNER MOULDINGS
Illus. 261

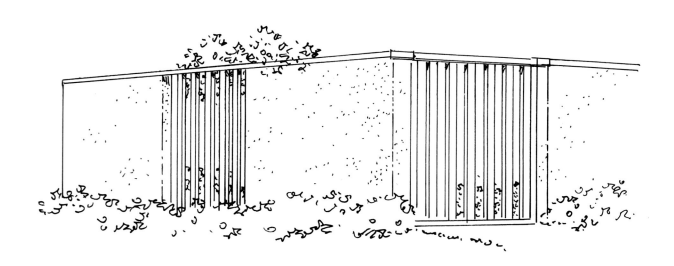

STUCCO CONCRETE WALL WITH SEE THRU WOOD SLATE INSERTS
Illus. 262

DESIGNER WROUGHT IRON
Illus. 263

WOOD PIER PILINGS WITH ANCHOR CHAIN
Illus. 264

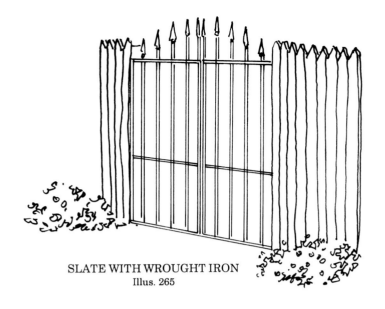

SLATE WITH WROUGHT IRON
Illus. 265

WHITE PICKET
Illus. 266

COLUMN SLATE
Illus. 267

Z-SHAPED WHITE PICKET
Illus. 268

NATURAL FLAGSTONE EDGED IN RED BRICK WITH BUILT IN BAR

Illus. 269

NATURAL FLAGSTONE EDGED IN RED BRICK WITH BUILT IN WOOD BENCH AND PLANTER

Illus. 270

CONCRETE PATIO EDGED IN RED BRICK WITH WOOD DECK ENTRANCE AND FLOWING ATTACHED POOL & SPA

Illus. 271

SLATE PATIO AND CIRCULAR PLANTER
Illus. 272

RED QUARRY TILE ACCENTED WITH CONCRETE EDGING SURROUNDED BY FLOWING WATER

Illus. 273

PATIOS AND DECKS

MULTILEVEL CONCRETE PATIO EDGED IN RED BRICK WITH BUILT IN PLANTERS

CURVED NATURAL FLAGSTONE WITH BUILT IN FOUNTAIN
Illus. 274

COMBINATION WOOD DECK & FLAGSTONE SURROUNDED BY WATER
Illus. 275

CONCRETE PATIO EDGED IN RED BRICK WITH NATURAL ROCK & STREAM

Illus. 276

PATIOS AND DECKS

WOOD DECK ACCENTED WITH BUILT IN BENCH AND PLANTERS
Illus. 277

MULTILEVEL RED QUARRY TILE WITH TWO TIERED STUCCO FOUNTAIN
Illus. 278

PATIOS AND DECKS

STUCCO WALL WITH ACRYLIC VIEW PANELS
Illus. 279

QUARRY TILE WITH STUCCO PLANTERS & STEEL GUARD RAILS
Illus. 280

GEOMETRIC SHAPED WOOD DECK WITH BUILT IN BENCHES
Illus. 281

WOOD DECK WITH SUNKEN BUILT IN SPA
Illus. 282

STAMPED CONCRETE EDGED IN BRICK
Illus. 283

MULTILEVEL WOOD DECK
Illus. 284

WOOD DECK CONNECTED BY A WALKWAY OVER A STREAM
Illus. 285

CORNER BENCH ON A WOOD DECK
Illus. 286

GEOMETRIC MULTILEVEL WOOD DECKING WITH DESIGNER HANDRAILS
Illus. 287

SMALL YARD SIMPLE WOOD DECK
Illus. 288

Z-SHAPED WOOD DECK BALCONY
Illus. 289

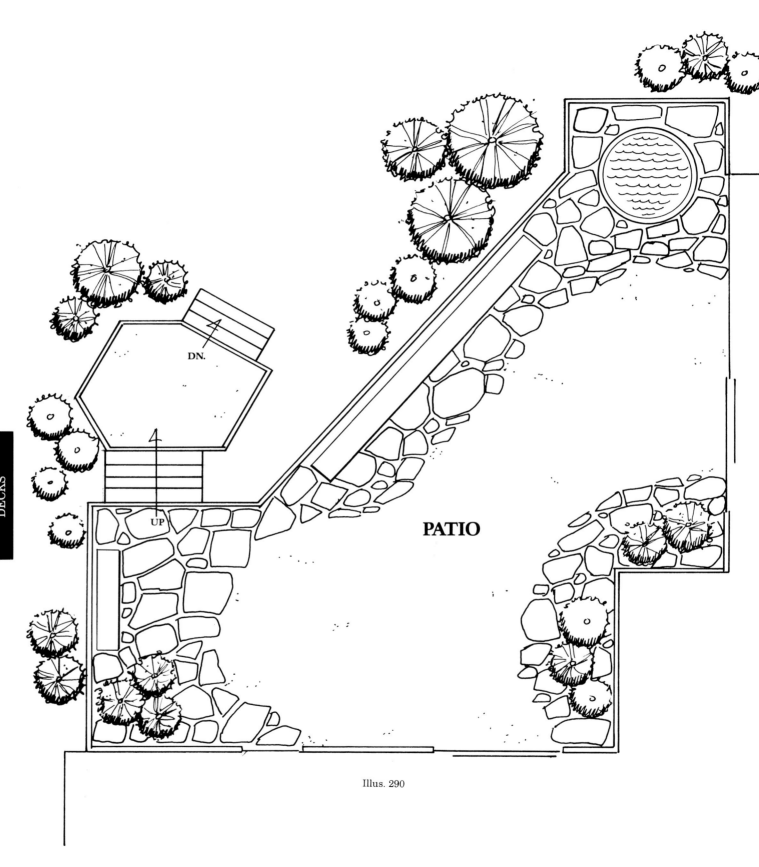

DN.

UP

PATIO

Illus. 290

PATIOS AND DECKS

Illus. 291

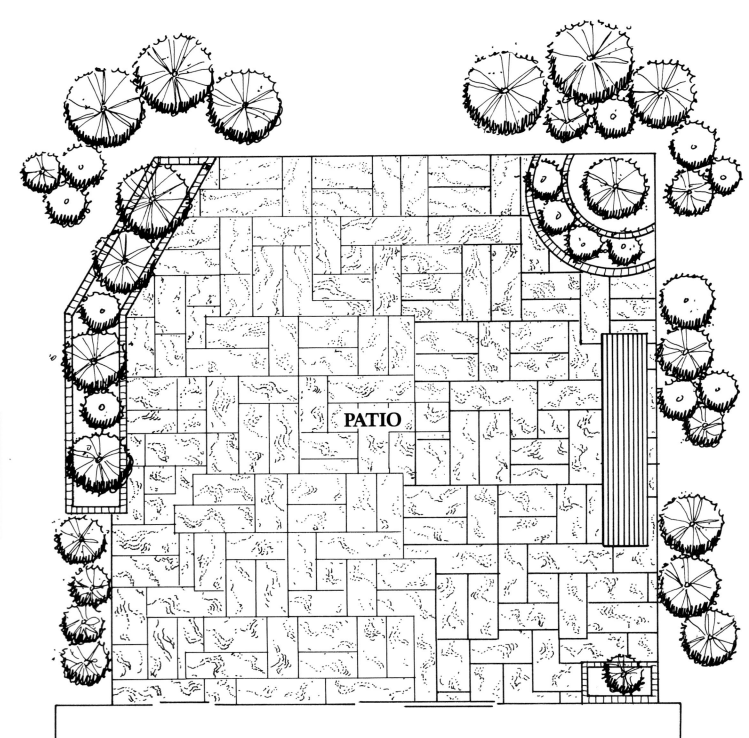

PATIO

Illus. 292

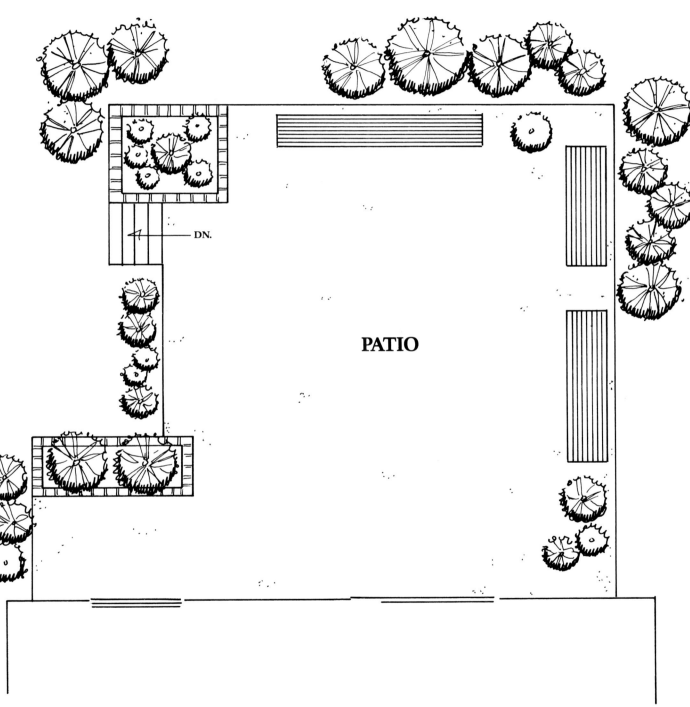

DN.

PATIO

Illus. 293

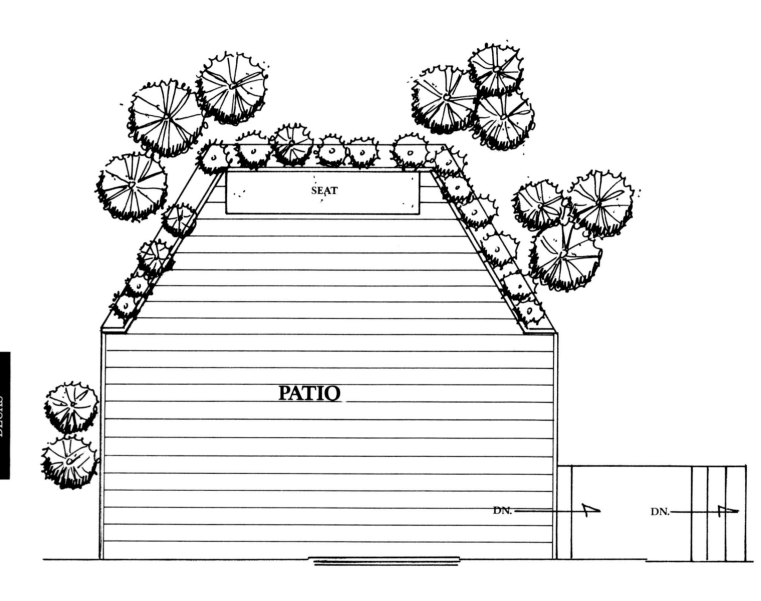

SEAT

PATIO

DN.

DN.

Illus. 294

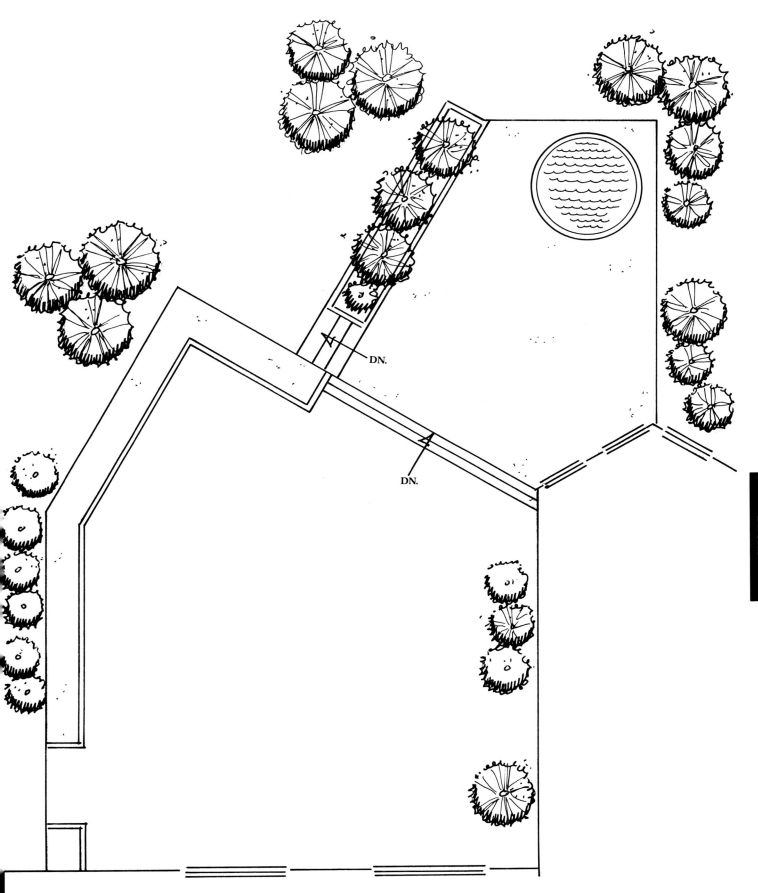

DN.

DN.

Illus. 295

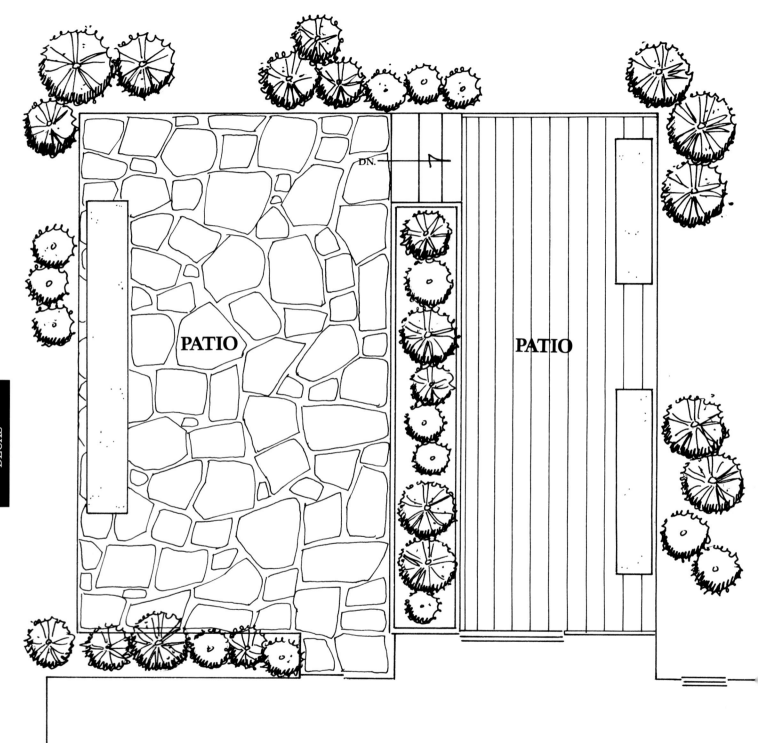

PATIO

PATIO

DN.

Illus. 296

PATIO COVERS & AWNINGS

FOUR COLUMN FREE STANDING COVER
Illus. 297

STUCCO COLUMN STRAIGHT BEAM COVER
Illus. 298

RUGGED SQUARE PATTERN COVER
Illus. 299

STAGGERED FIVE COLUMN OPEN AIR COVER
Illus. 300

MULTI CONFIGURED OPEN AIR AND LATTICE COVERED PATIO COVER
Illus. 301

SIX COLUMN FREE STANDING PYRAMID TOPPED COVER
Illus. 302

MULTILEVEL ABSTRACT COVER
Illus. 303

FOUR COLUMN OPEN AIR FREE STANDING COVER
Illus. 304

FIVE COLUMN OPEN AIR HEAVY BEAM DESIGNER COVER
Illus. 305

FOUR COLUMN HEAVY BEAM OPEN AIR FREE STANDING COVER
Illus. 306

DESIGNER DOUBLE BEAM ATTACHED COVER
Illus. 307

MULTILEVEL COLUMN FREE STANDING COVER
Illus. 308

LATTICE FREE STANDING COVER
Illus. 309

SPLIT LEVEL ATTACHED DOUBLE BEAM COVER
Illus.310

SINGLE LEVEL DOUBLE BEAM COVER WITH SIMPLE COLUMNS
Illus. 311

RIGHT ANGLE ATTACHED CLOSED COVER
Illus. 312

SINGLE LEVEL DOUBLE BEAM UNDER OPEN AIR COVER
Illus. 313

SPLIT LEVEL LATTICE ACCENTED COVER
Illus. 314

TRI LEVEL COVERED ATTACHED COVER
Illus. 315

FOUR COLUMN PYRAMID STYLE FREE STANDING COVER
Illus. 316

FREE STANDING LATTICE ENHANCED ARCHWAY COVER
Illus. 317

SOLID WOOD COVER WITH STAIRS TO DECK
Illus. 318

SOLID WOOD COVER WITH FRENCH DOORS TO DECK
Illus. 319

HEXAGON STYLE GAZEBO
Illus. 320

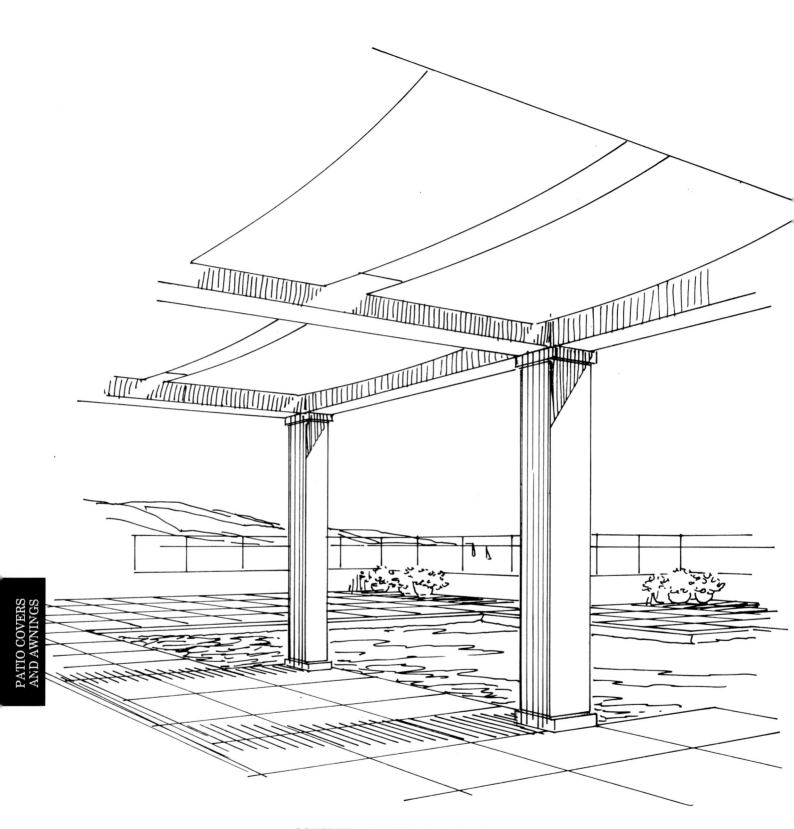

CONCRETE PILLARS WITH CANVAS COVER
Illus. 321

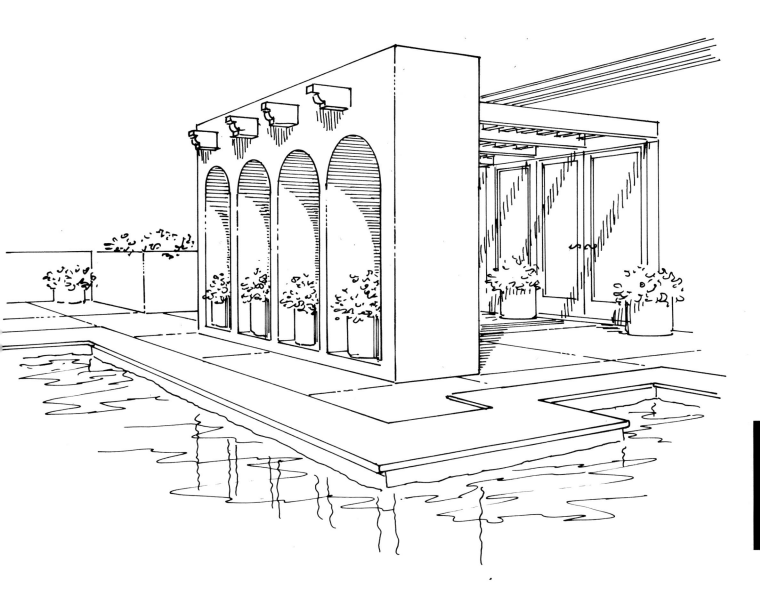

CONCRETE & STUCCO ARCHED ENTRYWAY SUPPORT COVER
Illus. 322

L-SHAPED COVERED SEATING AREA
Illus. 323

MULTI LATTICE WITH DESIGNER COLUMNS
Illus. 324

SIMPLE ATTACHED LATTICE COVER WITH FIRE RING
Illus. 325

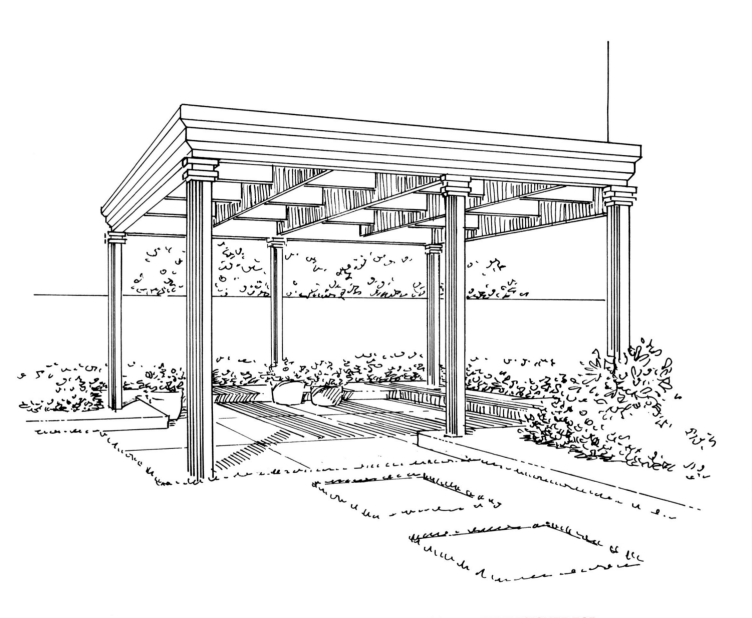

SIX COLUMN FREE STANDING HEAVY BEAM COVER WITH DESIGNER TOP
Illus. 326

MULTI BEAM FOUR COLUMN OPEN AIR GAZEBO
Illus.327

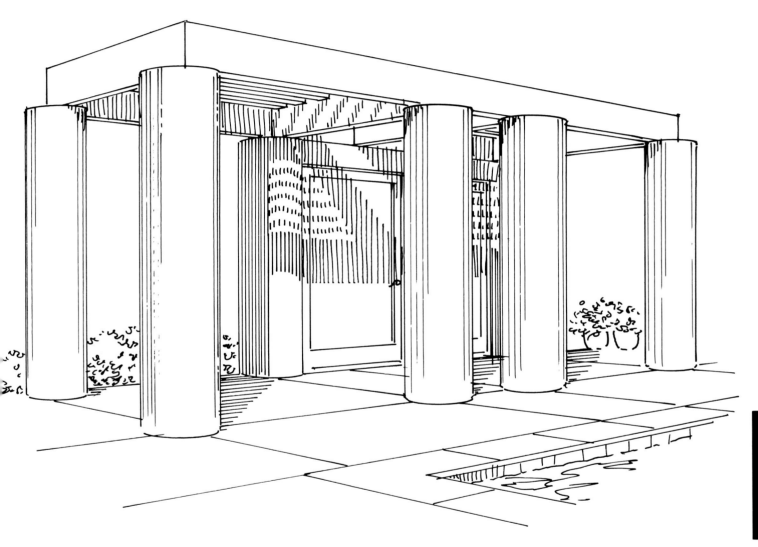

CONCRETE CYLINDER SUPPORTS WITH OPEN AIR COVER
Illus. 327

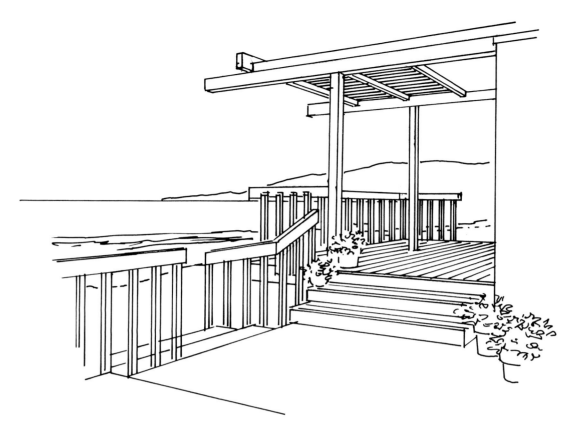

SIMPLE STRUT COVER WITH A WOOD DECK
Illus. 328

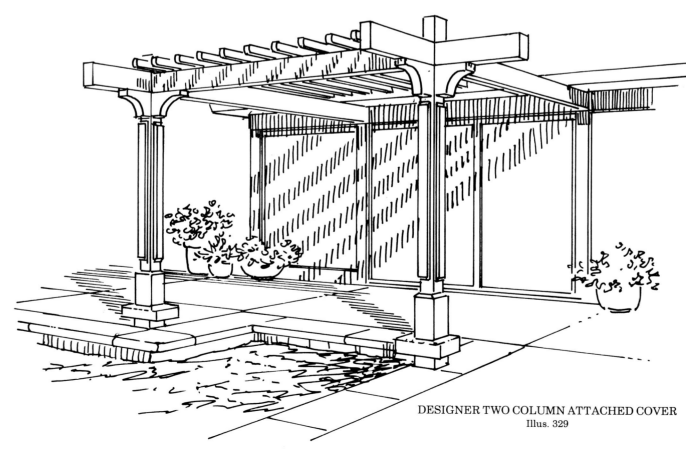

DESIGNER TWO COLUMN ATTACHED COVER
Illus. 329

LARGE OVERHEAD FOUR COLUMN FREE STANDING COVER
Illus. 330

ATTACHED MULTI STRUT COVER
Illus. 331

PYRAMID STYLE GAZEBO
Illus. 332

THREE SIDED LATTICE ENHANCED GAZEBO
Illus. 333

WOOD SHINGLE CONE STYLE HEXAGON GAZEBO
Illus. 334

WROUGHT IRON GAZEBO
Illus. 335

WOOD STYLE BENCHES

Illus. 336

Illus. 337

Illus. 338

Illus. 339

WOOD STYLE BENCHES

Illus. 340

Illus. 341

Illus. 342

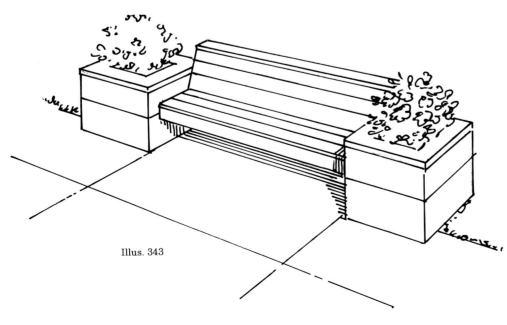

Illus. 343

DESIGNER PATIO COVER COLUMNS

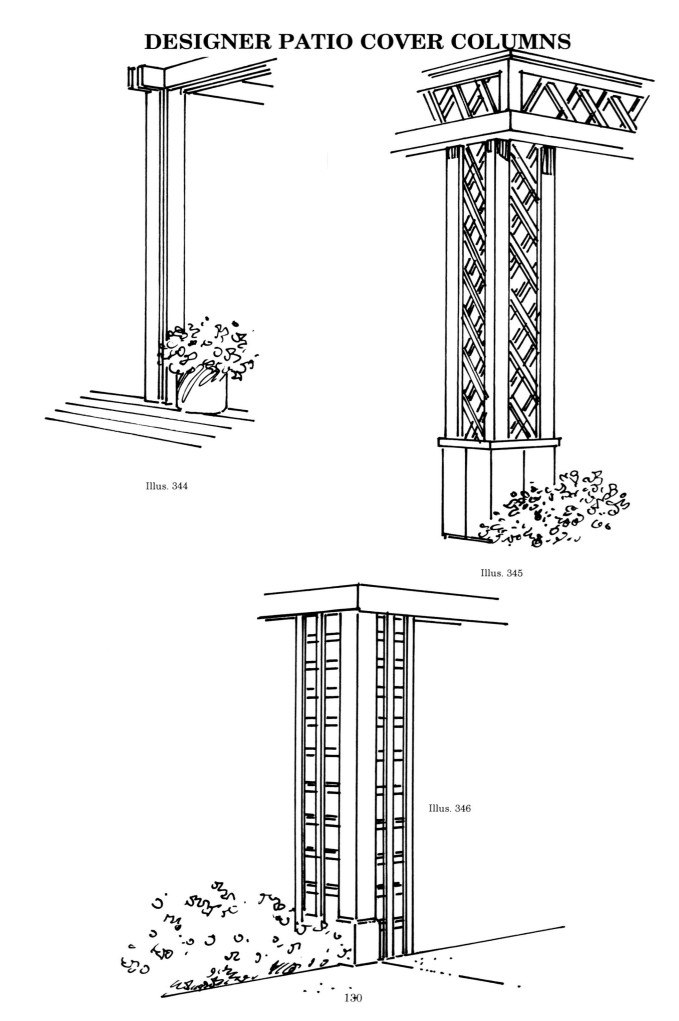

Illus. 344

Illus. 345

Illus. 346

DESIGNER PATIO COVER COLUMNS

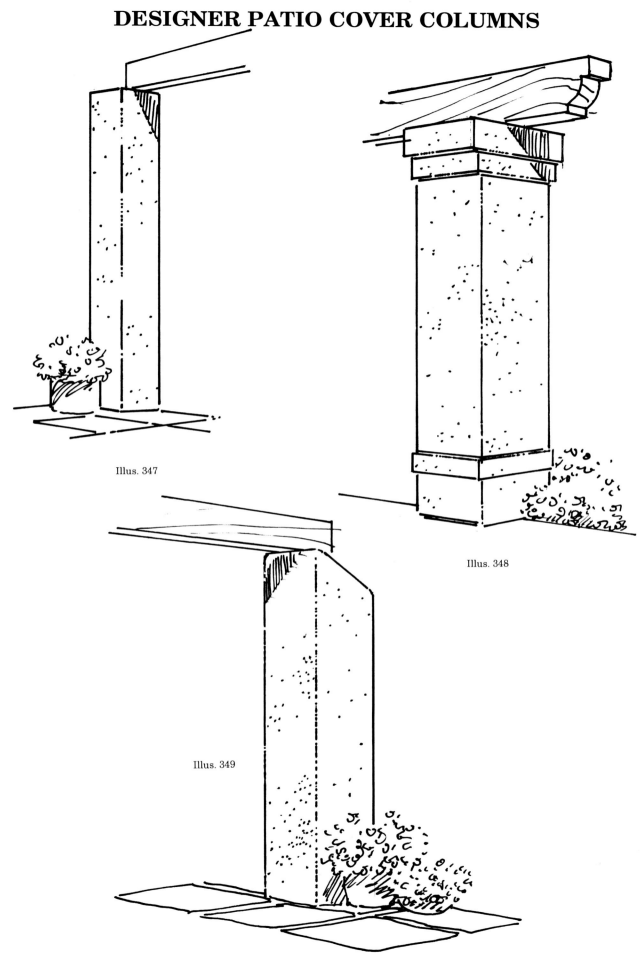

Illus. 347

Illus. 348

Illus. 349

DESIGNER PATIO COVER COLUMNS

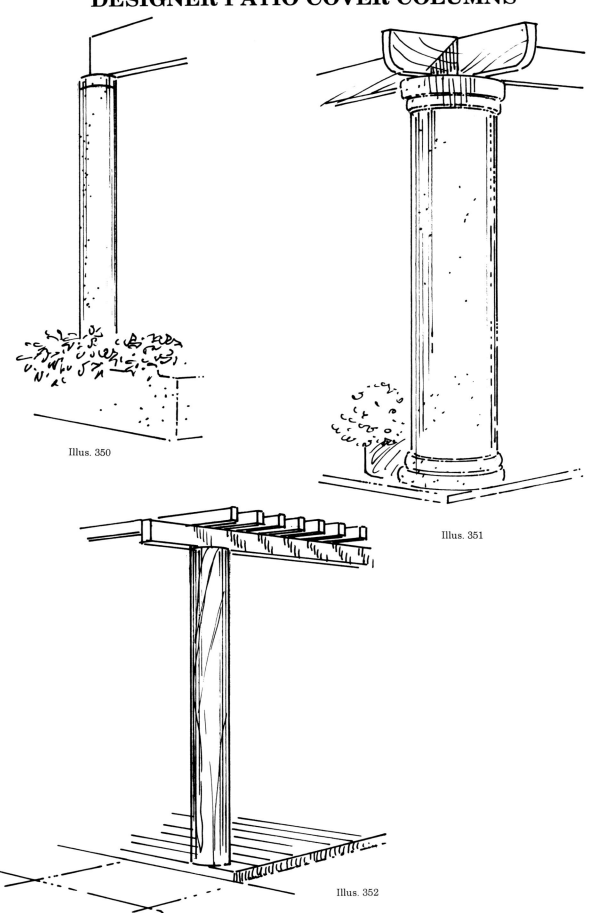

Illus. 350

Illus. 351

Illus. 352

DESIGNER PATIO COVER COLUMNS

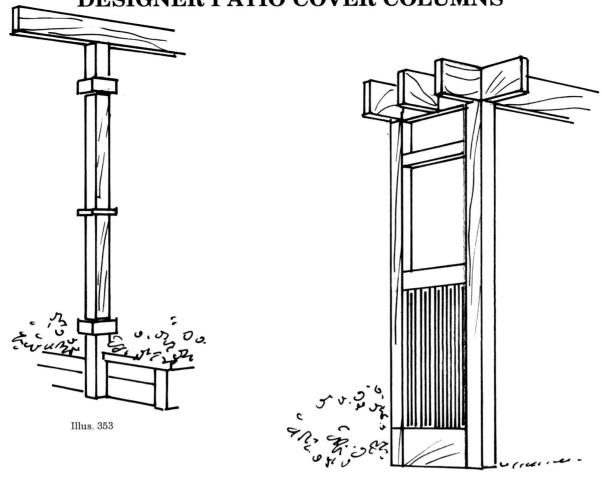

Illus. 353

Illus. 354

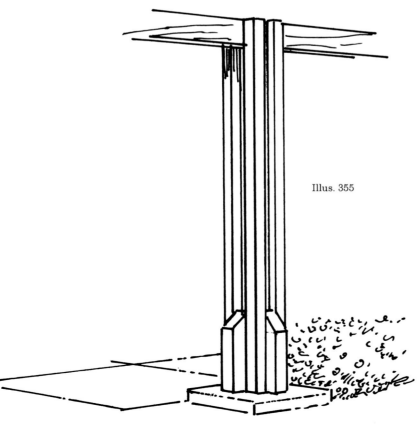

Illus. 355

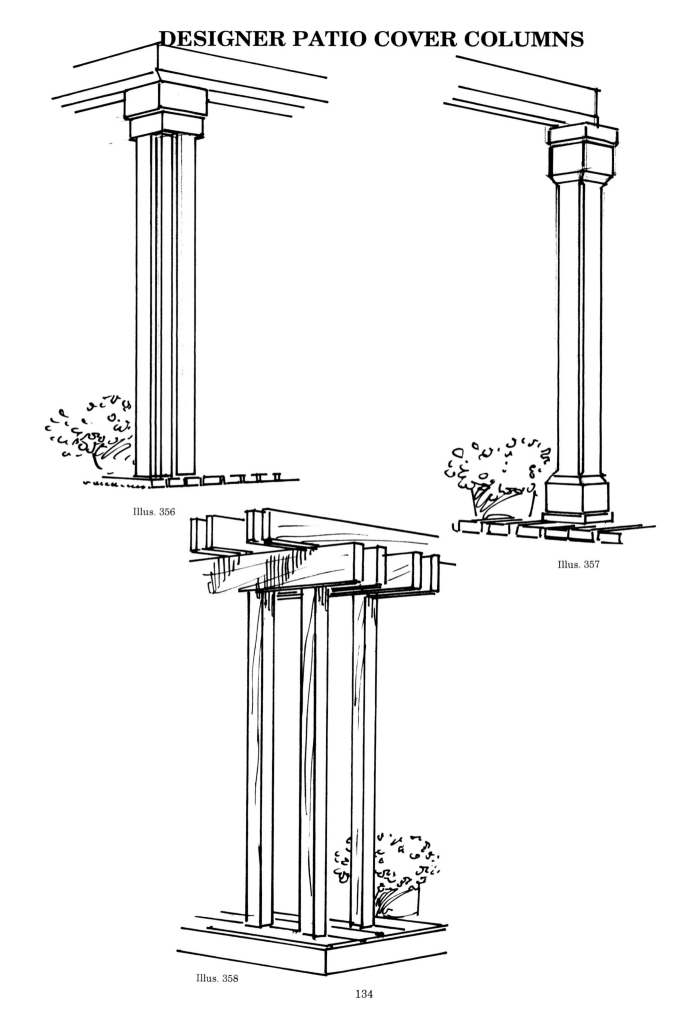

Illus. 356

Illus. 357

Illus. 358

DESIGNER PATIO COVER COLUMNS

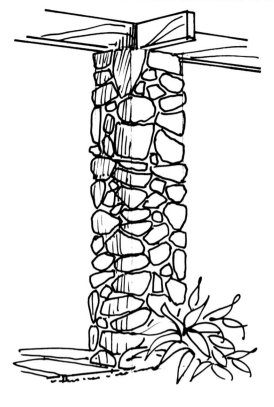

Illus. 359

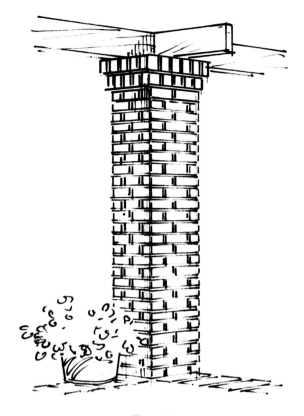

Illus. 360

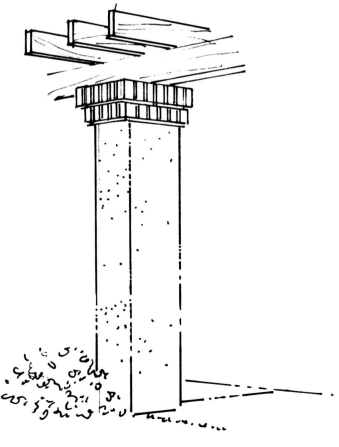

Illus. 361

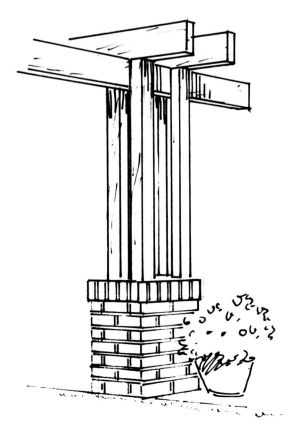

Illus. 362

CORBEL ENDS

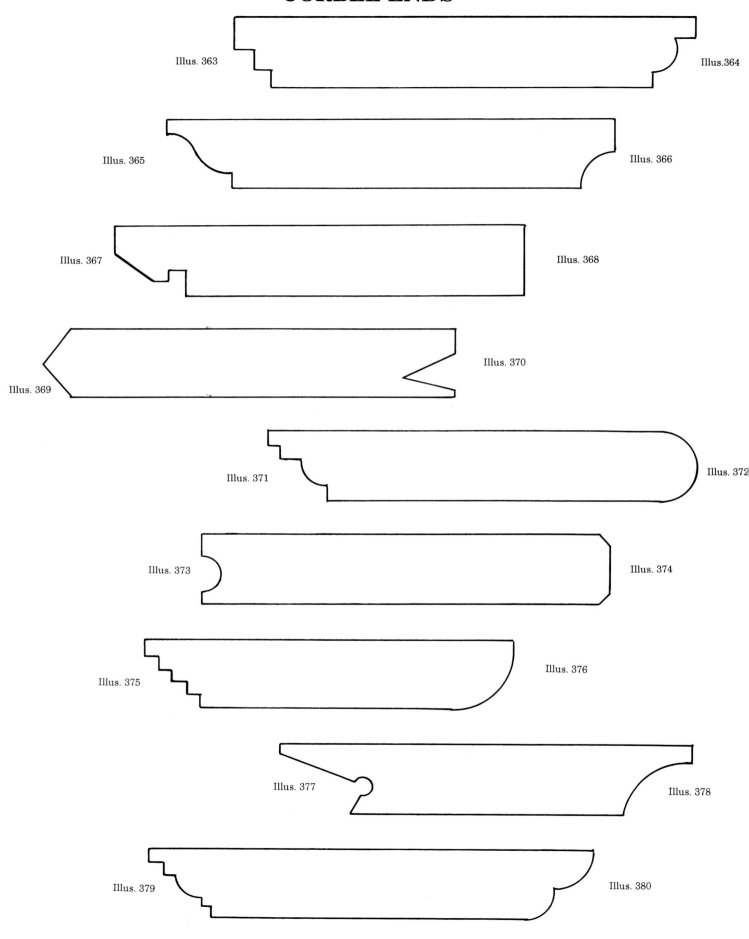

Illus. 363

Illus.364

Illus. 365

Illus. 366

Illus. 367

Illus. 368

Illus. 370

Illus. 369

Illus. 371

Illus. 372

Illus. 373

Illus. 374

Illus. 375

Illus. 376

Illus. 377

Illus. 378

Illus. 379

Illus. 380

WATER FALLS & PONDS

PLASTER FOUNTAIN SET IN STUCCO CIRCULAR PLANTERS
Illus. 381

PLASTER FOUNTAIN SET IN RED BRICK PLANTERS
Illus. 382

PLASTER STYLE FOUNTAINS WITH BRICK POOL
Illus. 383

NATURAL RIVER ROCK FOUNTAIN
Illus. 384

ROCK WATERFALL FLOWING INTO A MULTILEVEL CONCRETE POND
Illus. 385

TRIANGULAR STUCCO & BRICK FOUNTAIN
Illus. 386

NATURAL ROCK WATERFALL
Illus. 387

ROCK FOUNTAIN WATERFALL FLOWING INTO A CURVED STREAM
Illus. 388

LARGE ROCK GEOMETRIC SHAPED WATERFALL
Illus. 389

SIMULATED ROCK LARGE VOLUME WATERFALL
Illus. 390

SIMULATED ROCK MULTI LEVEL WATERFALL
Illus. 391

LARGE POND WITH CENTER FOUNTAIN
Illus. 392

CONCRETE AND TILE WATERFALL FLOWING INTO SPA
Illus. 393

SMOOTH CONCRETE CENTER EDGED WITH STAMPED CONCRETE
Illus. 394

SMOOTH CONCRETE CENTER EDGED IN RED BRICK
Illus. 395

AGGREGATE CONCRETE CENTER EDGED WITH RED BRICK
Illus. 396

SMALL ROCK AGGREGATE CENTER EDGED IN LARGE ROCK AGGREGATE
Illus. 397

RED BRICK CENTER EDGED IN AGGREGATE CONCRETE
Illus. 398

QUARRY TILE CENTER EDGED IN AGGREGATE CONCRETE
Illus. 399

BRUSH FINISH CONCRETE
Illus. 400

ROCK SALT FINISH CONCRETE
Illus. 401

AGGREGATE ROCK CONCRETE
Illus. 402

ROCK SALT FINISH CONCRETE CENTER EDGED IN BROWN BRICK
Illus. 403

ROCK SALT FINISH CONCRETE EDGED WITH WOOD
Illus. 404

STAMPED CONCRETE PADS SURROUNDED WITH SMOOTH ROCK
Illus. 405

RED BRICK STEPS EDGED IN WOOD
Illus. 406

COLORED CONCRETE STEPS DOWN TO A WOOD DECK
Illus. 407

COMBINATION ROCK & FLAGSTONE WALKWAY
Illus. 408

NATURAL FLAGSTONE
Illus. 409

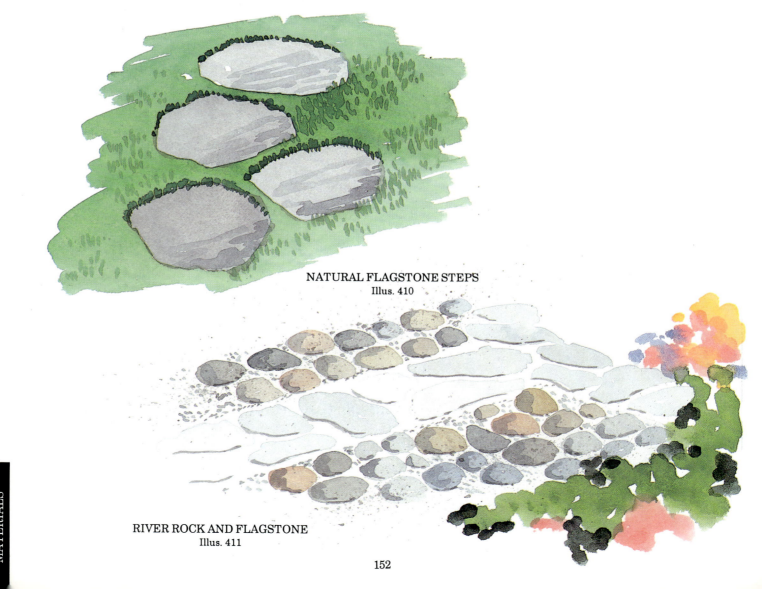

NATURAL FLAGSTONE STEPS
Illus. 410

RIVER ROCK AND FLAGSTONE
Illus. 411

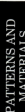

STAMPED CONCRETE
Illus. 412

COBBLESTONE EDGED WITH FLAGSTONE
Illus. 413

COBBLESTONE FINISH
Illus. 414

HEXAGON QUARRY TILE FINISH
Illus. 415

ASSORTED STONE FINISHES

Illus. 416

Illus. 417

Illus. 418

ASSORTED STONE FINISHES

Illus. 419

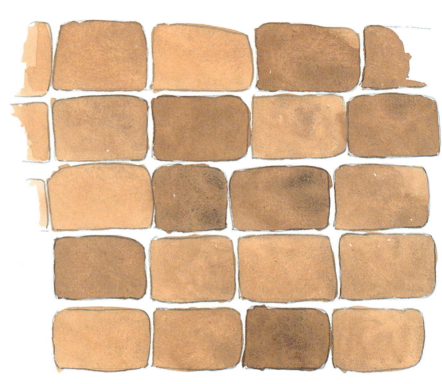

Illus. 420

Illus. 421

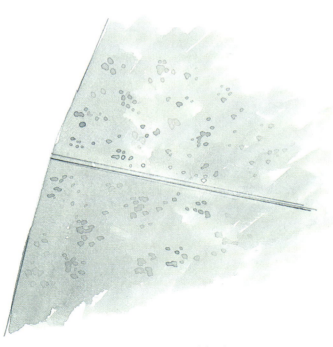

COLORED STAMPED CONCRETE
Illus. 422

ROCK SALT FINISH CONCRETE
Illus. 423

ASSORTED ROCK FINISHES

Illus. 424

Illus. 425

Illus. 427

Illus. 426

TWO TONE BRICK PATTERNS

Illus. 428

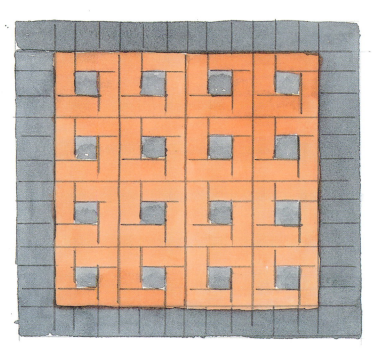

Illus. 429

ASSORTED BRICK PATTERN

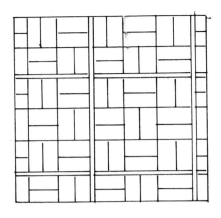

DIVIDED HALF BASKET WEAVE
Illus. 430

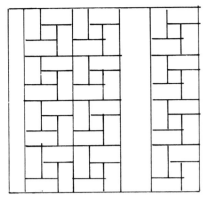

DIVIDED PINWHEEL
Illus. 431

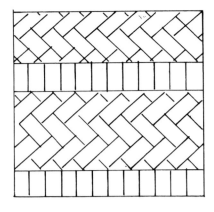

DIVIDED HERRINGBONE
Illus. 432

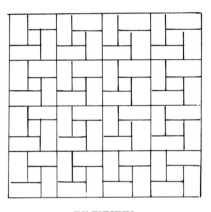

PINWHEEL
Illus. 433

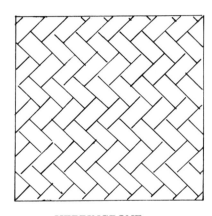

HERRINGBONE
Illus. 434

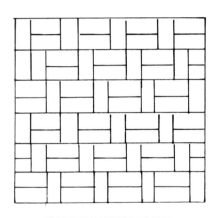

HALF BASKET WEAVE
Illus. 435

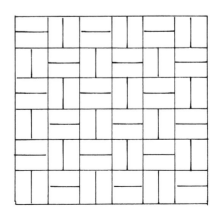

BASKET WEAVE
Illus. 436

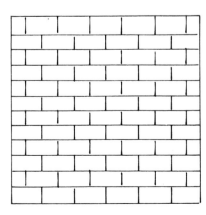

RUNNING BOND
Illus. 437

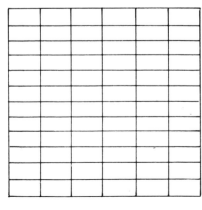

JACK ON JACK
Illus. 438